Sports Stars

LYNETTE WOODARD

The First Female Globetrotter

By Bert Rosenthal

CP CHILDRENS PRESS ®

CHICAGO

Cover photograph: Bryan Yablonsky
Inside photographs courtesy of the following:
Bryan Yablonsky, pages 6, 22, 28, and 44
Ira Golden, pages 9, 11, 13, 20, 24, 26, 31, 33, 35, 37,
39, and 42
Kansas University, pages 14, 16, and 18

Library of Congress Cataloging in Publication Data

Rosenthal, Bert.
  Lynette Woodard: the first female Globetrotter.

  (Sport stars)
  Summary: Follows the life and career of the individual who
made sports history by becoming the first woman to play
basketball for the Harlem Globetrotters.
  1. Woodard, Lynette—Juvenile literature. 2. Basketball
players—United States—Biography—Juvenile literature.
3. Harlem Globetrotters—Juvenile literature.
[1. Woodard, Lynette. 2. Women basketball players.
3. Basketball players. 4. Afro-Americans—Biography]
I. Title. II. Series.
GV884.W63R67 1986   796.32'3'0924 [B] [92] 86-9662
ISBN 0-516-04360-9

  2 3 4 5 6 7 8 9 10 R 95, 94, 93, 92, 91 90 ‹

Sports Stars

LYNETTE WOODARD

The First Female Globetrotter

Lynette Woodard has made sports history.

She did it by becoming the first woman to play basketball for the Harlem Globetrotters.

From 1927, when the team was formed, until 1985, no woman had played for the Globetrotters. Lynette became the first.

The team decided it needed some new spark. So she got her chance. For 59 years, the Globetrotters had been entertaining people throughout the world. Their basketball playing was fun. However, their act was growing old. They needed some new life.

So, team president Earl Duryea decided to hire a woman. It was a bold move. Some of the players on the team weren't sure. They didn't know if a woman would fit in on the all-men's team.

That didn't bother Mr. Duryea. He was certain. A woman was what the Globetrotters needed.

Lynette and teammate Billy Ray Hobley

Lynette had dreamed for a long time about playing for the Globetrotters. But she never thought that dream would come true.

The dream began when she was about five years old. Lynette first heard of the Globetrotters at that age. She was told about the team by her cousin, Geese Ausbie.

Geese also was a member of the Globetrotters. One night, he came to Lynette's house for dinner. While there, he began twirling a basketball on his finger. Lynette loved watching Geese do tricks with the ball.

"It was unreal," she said. "I couldn't believe the magnificent things he was doing with a basketball."

Lynette tried some of the tricks. She wasn't very successful. In fact, she broke some things in the house while trying to imitate what Geese did.

Nevertheless, Lynette still dreamed about being a Globetrotter.

First, though, she had to become a very good woman's basketball player. So, she practiced playing basketball for many hours in her hometown of Wichita, Kansas.

Steve Schmidt of the Washington Generals tries to dribble past Lynette.

Lynette at Kansas University

By the time she got to Kansas University, she was an excellent player. She attended Kansas from 1977 to 1981. During that time, she won many honors.

In 1979, she was selected to play on the United States team that competed in the Spartakiade Games in the Soviet Union. That team also played in the World University Games. They won the gold medal.

In 1980, Lynette was selected as a member of the United States Olympic team. That team, however, did not compete in the Olympic Games. The 1980 Olympics were held in Moscow, the capital city of the Soviet Union.

At that time, the United States and the Soviet Union were not on friendly terms. So, the United States decided not to attend the Olympic Games.

While at Kansas, Lynette also became the highest-scoring woman's college basketball player in history. She finished her career with 3,649 points. As a freshman, she averaged 25.2 points per game. As a sophomore, she averaged 31. As a junior, she averaged 23.8. And as a senior, she averaged 24.5.

As a Kansas University basketball player, Lynette broke the women's career scoring record.

On January 6, 1981, she broke the women's career scoring record. That record—3,199 points—was held by Carol Blazejowski of Montclair State. The record-breaking points came on her first basket during a game against Stephen F. Austin College.

Lynette finished her college career with a scoring average of 26.3 points a game. She had an average of 12.3 rebounds a game. She also led the nation in steals each of her last three years. And she was tops on her team in assists for four straight years.

Lynette was described by her coach, Marian Washington, as a player "who can do it all."

Lynette and some of her trophies

After her senior year, Lynette was named winner of the Wade Trophy. The trophy is given to the outstanding player in women's college basketball.

When she received the trophy, Lynette said she wanted to continue playing basketball in the Women's Basketball League. The league collapsed because of money problems. So Lynette went to Italy to play basketball. She stayed there one year.

She then returned to the United States. In 1983, she played on the United States team that won the gold medal in the Pan American Games.

Lynette said she never thought about gender, she just wanted to play for the Globetrotters.

She also played on the 1983 U.S. team. They won the silver medal in the World University Games.

In 1984, Lynette became a member of the United States Olympic team again. She was elected team captain. The team won the gold medal in the Olympic Games in Los Angeles.

After the games, she was a woman without a team again. Still, she dreamed of playing for the Globetrotters. While in college, Lynette had written cousin Geese. She asked him what her chances were of becoming a Globetrotter.

To become a Globetrotter, Lynette competed with 17 of the best women athletes.

"I never thought about gender [men or women]," she said. "I just knew that I wanted to play for the Globetrotters."

Instead, she had to get another job. She became an assistant coach at her old school, Kansas.

Then, one day in 1983, she saw an advertisement in a newspaper. The ad said the Globetrotters would be holding tryouts for women players. They would sign one player. She was shocked and happy.

"My immediate thought was, 'You don't have to look any further.'" Lynette said. "I got on the telephone right away and called the Harlem Globetrotters and they said it was for real."

The team held two tryout camps. The first was in Charlotte, North Carolina, in July 1985.

Richard Miller is one of the game officials.

The second was in Burbank, California, in October 1985.

A total of 18 women were selected for the tryout camps. Among the women were twins Pam and Paula McGee, both of whom attended the University of Southern California. The group also included Joyce Walker of Louisiana State and Sandra Hodge of the University of New Orleans.

They were the best women players in the country. None was better than Lynette. When the tryouts ended, she was the one chosen to join the Globetrotters. Her dream had come true.

Lynette waves to the fans.

"It's a wonderful feeling," Lynette said. "I'm so excited I can't hide it.

"There's a lot to be learned, and I'm ready to work hard," she added. "I have the basic skills to be a part of this team."

While Lynette was becoming an important part of the team, another important part was missing. Her cousin, Geese, had left the Globetrotters after a dispute with management.

Geese had played for the team for 24 years. Lynette was sad for Geese. But she was happy for herself.

Sweet Lou Dunbar has been playing with the Globetrotters for about 10 years.

The other players also were unhappy to see Geese leave. And they were unsure about Lynette.

"It was a shock," said Sweet Lou Dunbar, the team's clown prince. "My first reaction was: Show me, don't tell me. I figured it might be a publicity stunt."

"This seemed like just another gimmick," said Larry "Gator' Rivers, who assisted Coach Russell Ellington at the first trials.

Lynette quickly proved to the men that she could play. It didn't take her long to win their respect.

She was helped by her cousin Geese. Even though he no longer was on the team, he encouraged her.

"He's been very special to me," she said.

Ten days after Lynette joined the team, she played her first game with the Globetrotters. That was on October 17, 1985, in Brisbane, Australia.

Four weeks later, she played her first game as a member of the Globetrotters in the United States. That game was in Spokane, Washington.

In January 1986, she made her first live television appearance as a member of the team.

Frank Beretta of the Washington Generals guards Lynette.

That was in a game at Kansas City, near her Wichita home. A month later, she played in Wichita.

The Globetrotters travel constantly. It's a tough schedule. Sometimes, the team plays two games in two cities on the same day.

Coach Ellington liked the way Lynette adjusted to the team.

"I think she has what we're looking for," he said. "She has talent. She has congeniality. She loves doing what she's doing, and you have to do that to play some 200 games a year. If you don't love it, it gets to you sometimes."

Lynette and Head Coach Russell Ellington watch from the sidelines.

Lynette agreed with her coach. "You can't like it, you've got to love it," she said.

"I love it," she added. "My dream has become my reality. The playing is fun. And entertaining audiences and creating laughter and bringing joy to people . . . there's a lot of positive energy that flows during a game.

"I enjoy that. I'm always seeing happy people, friendly people. And who wouldn't enjoy that?

"Sometimes it just doesn't seem real," Lynette continued. "How many people get to do what they always dreamed of doing? It's an honor, a privilege. This is the opportunity of the century, the first time in history.

The Globetrotters make the audience, and themselves, laugh during their
games.

"I'm having a great time. But you have to be aware of where you are, that it's a show. I'm in an arena where I can do crazy things, things I've always wanted to do. In a regular game, I wouldn't even think of trying them."

The Globetrotters play the game mostly for fun. They want to entertain the millions of fans who watch them all over the world, in person and on television. Winning is secondary. Winning also is expected.

The Globetrotters have not lost a game since January 5, 1971. That's when they were beaten 100 to 99 by the Washington Generals. Since then, the Generals, the Globetrotters' opponents every game, have been losers.

The last time the Globetrotters lost was in 1971.

"You don't start out playing **the game competi**tively," Lynette said. "I didn't. It's **fun. Then, it** turned into something for a while that **wasn't** fun. If you lost, ugh, it wasn't fun.

"But I've always played for the joy of the game. What this [playing for the Globetrotters] has done is put me back in my natural state. This is relaxed," she said. "We're having fun. We're bringing joy to people's lives in a unique way, through our basketball talent.

"At the Olympics, you have more of a competitive spirit. All you think about is winning. You don't think about pleasing anybody else except that win column."

Lynette has fans everywhere and she takes time to be with them. Here she visits with girlscouts from Greater New York.

Since becoming a Globetrotter, Lynette has been very busy. A typical week includes eight games in seven cities. In between, she gives many newspaper and television interviews. And before and after each game, she spends about 20 minutes signing autographs.

"I get a lot of calls from fans," she said. "They tell me they saw the game and how much they liked my being in it. And the kids make signs for me.

"I don't think anybody's ever been on a schedule like this—unless they've played for the Globetrotters.

"I wouldn't trade it for anything, though," she said.

In her early days with the team, Lynette had a lot to learn.

"There are so many routines in the show to learn," she explained. "There are so many things to get the audience to respond. Making people laugh is the greatest feeling. With all the terrible things that go on in the world, it's nice to be able to make people forget them and laugh for a few hours."

Making people happy obviously is part of Lynette's game. She does it with her basketball

Lynette is still scoring points.

talent, her personality, and her beautiful smile that could melt butter.

"Globetrotters don't just play," said James "Twiggy" Sanders, a long-time member of the team. "They've got to have fun and project that fun into the crowd. Lynette really helps break the monotony. She comes to play, and she comes to have fun."

Although Lynette is a pioneer in women's athletics, she doesn't feel like one.

"I'm just doing what I love to do, and that's where I leave it," she said.

Lynette said she hopes the publicity she is receiving as a member of the Globetrotters will help other women players.

Lynette's dream has come true.

"I hope it helps a women's professional basketball league become viable and stable," she said. "There are a lot of other women who had the same dream I had, but they don't have any place to go after their college days."

In 1986, Lynette worked hard on her ball-handling skills. She got better and better. She got so good she was added to the Magic Circle. That means she is now one of the best Globetrotters. Before each game, she and four other players do tricks with the ball. Lynette is very honored to be a part of the Magic Circle.

Her team also traveled to Europe in 1986. Throughout North America and Europe, the team played games in more than 80 cities.

And Lynette got another surprise. She was joined by another woman on the Globetrotters. Jackie White of Fresno, California, a basketball star at Long Beach State University, is now the second woman on the team. Lynette and Jackie are both guards.

But Lynette will always be No. 1—the first woman to play for the Harlem Globetrotters. It was a place she dreamed about for many years. Her dream came true.

CHRONOLOGY

1977—Lynette enters Kansas University.

1978—For the first of four consecutive years, Lynette is named to the All-American team.

1979—Lynette plays on the United States team that wins the gold medal in the World University Games.

1980—Lynette is chosen as a member of the United States Olympic team.

1981—Lynette is selected as Outstanding Female of the Year in the Big Eight Conference, Woman of the Year by the NAACP chapter of Wichita, Kansas, and winner of the Wade Trophy as the outstanding women's college basketball player.

—On January 6, Lynette becomes the leading all-time scorer in women's college basketball. With her first field goal during a game against Stephen F. Austin College, she surpasses the record of 3,199 points held by Carol Blazejowski of Montclair State. Lynette finishes her collegiate career with 3,649 points—the most by a man or woman in Kansas University history.

1982—Lynette spends the year playing basketball in Italy.

1983—Lynette plays on the United States team that wins the gold medal in the Pan American Games and the silver medal in the World University Games.

1984—For the second time Lynette makes the U.S. Olympic team and is named captain. The team wins the Olympic gold medal.

1985—Lynette beats out 17 other women for a spot on the Harlem Globetrotters, a team that had been all male in the past. On October 17, she makes her debut with the Globetrotters in a game at Brisbane, Australia.

1986—A game at Spokane, Washington, marks Lynette's U.S. debut with the Globetrotters. Later, she makes her U.S. television debut with the Globetrotters in a game at Kansas City, and plays in her hometown of Wichita, Kansas.

—Lynette receives a citation from the President of the United States on National Women's Sports Day, February 4.

—With the Globetrotterss, Lynette travels to Europe to play.

—Jackie White of Long Beach State joins the Globetrotters as the second woman on the team. Lynette has proved a woman is a good addition to the team.

—Lynette joins the Globetrotters' summer camp staff.

ABOUT THE AUTHOR

Bert Rosenthal has worked for The Associated Press for more than 25 years. He has covered or written about virtually every sport. Mr. Rosenthal is the author of Sports Stars books on Larry Bird, Marques Johnson, Sugar Ray Leonard, Darryl Dawkins, Wayne Gretzky, Isiah Thomas, Carl Lewis, Ralph Sampson, and Dwight Gooden. He is also the author of New True Books of Soccer and Basketball.

He was AP's pro basketball editor from 1973 until 1976. From 1974 until 1980, he was the secretary-treasurer of the Professional Basketball Writers' Association of America. He has been a coauthor on two books—*Pro Basketball Superstars of 1974* and *Pro Basketball Superstars of 1975*. For seven years, Mr. Rosenthal was the editor of *Hoop Magazine*, an official publication of the National Basketball Association.

At present, he is AP's track and field editor, and a frequent contributor to many basketball, football, and baseball magazines. He also has covered three Olympic Games: the 1976 Olympics in Montreal, the 1980 Games in Moscow, and the 1984 Olympics in Los Angeles.